BEASTLY BIBLE STORIES

Troublemaking Teacher

CLAIRE BENTON-EVANS

BEASTLY BIBLE STORIES

Troublemaking Teacher

Illustrations by Tim Benton

kevin
mayhew

www.kevinmayhew.com

kevin
mayhew

First published in Great Britain in 2014 by Kevin Mayhew Ltd
Buxhall, Stowmarket, Suffolk IP14 3BW
Tel: +44 (0) 1449 737978 Fax: +44 (0) 1449 737834
E-mail: info@kevinmayhew.com

www.kevinmayhew.com

ISBN 978 1 84867 750 0
Catalogue No. 1501461

Cover design by Rob Mortonson
Illustrations by Tim Benton
Edited by Nicki Copeland
Typeset by Richard Weaver

Printed and bound in Great Britain

CONTENTS

ABOUT THE AUTHOR

Claire loves stories and drama but she never once played the Angel Gabriel in a school Nativity play. She studied English at Oxford, where she enjoyed reading lots of very old poems about monsters, battles and God. She gets her best ideas for writing when she's walking her dog and loves living in Scotland because she likes shortbread and mountains. She lives with her husband – a minister – and three children. They all have their own big ideas about church and they dared her to write **Beastly Bible Stories**.

Details of all Claire's titles can be found on her website at:

www.clairebentonevans.com

www.kevinmayhew.com

UNCLEAN AND UNWELCOME
Jesus heals lepers and a Samaritan

A disgusting disease

'**LORD! LOOK OUT! LEPERS!**' The disciples pointed in terror at the ten stooped and bandaged men in the distance. They could smell their filthy rags and hear their hoarse cry: '**UNCLEAN! UNCLEAN!**' Jesus ignored his friends' panic and pressed on towards the poor lads with leprosy.

LEPROSY – the word alone made people in Jesus' time want to wash their hands. They were terrified of catching this disease because of what it does to you: it makes your skin go scaly and lumpy like tree bark, it hurts your eyes so that you can't see and it makes breathing hard. Bits of your body go knobbly and numb. Today we have drugs that cure leprosy,* but in Jesus' time nothing could make you better. And the illness itself wasn't the end of your misfortune. Here are the Bible's rules about what to do if you reckoned you had leprosy:

---

* In the past 20 years, 16 million people across the world have been cured of leprosy!

- Go and get yourself checked by the priest.

- If you have leprosy, the priest will label you '**UNCLEAN**'.

- You must wear torn clothes, have messy hair and wear a mask over your mouth.

- Wherever you go, you must yell, '**UNCLEAN! UNCLEAN!**' to warn other people to get out of your way.

- You must live alone – leave your home and family and go and live away from everyone else.

People who suffered from leprosy in Jesus' time were called lepers, as if they were no longer people at all, and they lived together in groups. Everyone else avoided lepers like the plague – which was exactly what people thought leprosy was. They were scared of the thought of it and sickened by the sight of it – they believed they could catch it just by standing near a sufferer.*

Unclean and unwelcome

The lepers lurched closer. While Jesus' disciples stood rooted to the spot, squeamish and scared, Jesus himself strode towards the ten suffering men. Nine of them were Jews but the tenth was a Samaritan, which made him doubly unwelcome: everyone excluded him because of his leprosy, and the Jews thought that all Samaritans were rotten, revolting and wrong about religion. Even the other lepers left the Samaritan out. No one talked to him at all.

* You can't – it's not very infectious.

10

As Jesus came closer, the men recognised him – he was famous for his healing miracles! He was their only hope! '**JESUS!**' they yelled. '**MASTER! HAVE PITY ON US!**'

Jesus looked at the ten men with their rags and their stumpy fingers and their sore, lumpy skin. He didn't shudder. He didn't look away. He saw ten twisted faces raised hopefully in his direction and he said, 'Go and let the priest have a look at you.' The men's hopeful faces fell and their shoulders sagged. So Jesus wasn't going to make them better after all – he was simply sending them to the priest to be labelled '**UNCLEAN**', and they knew that already. The men turned and hobbled away. Jesus watched them go.

Ten seconds later, one leper said, 'I can feel my feet!'

Half a minute after that, a second leper said, 'I can see properly!'

A third shouted, 'It doesn't hurt when I breathe!'

'Look!' yelled a fourth, 'My legs! The skin's gone all smooth!'

'Look at my arms!' cried the fifth. 'There are no lumps and bumps!'

'My sores are healing!' whooped the sixth.

'My legs feel stronger than ever!' screamed the seventh.

'I don't need these bandages any more!' exclaimed the eighth.

'**MY FINGERS ARE GROWING BACK!**' bellowed the ninth.

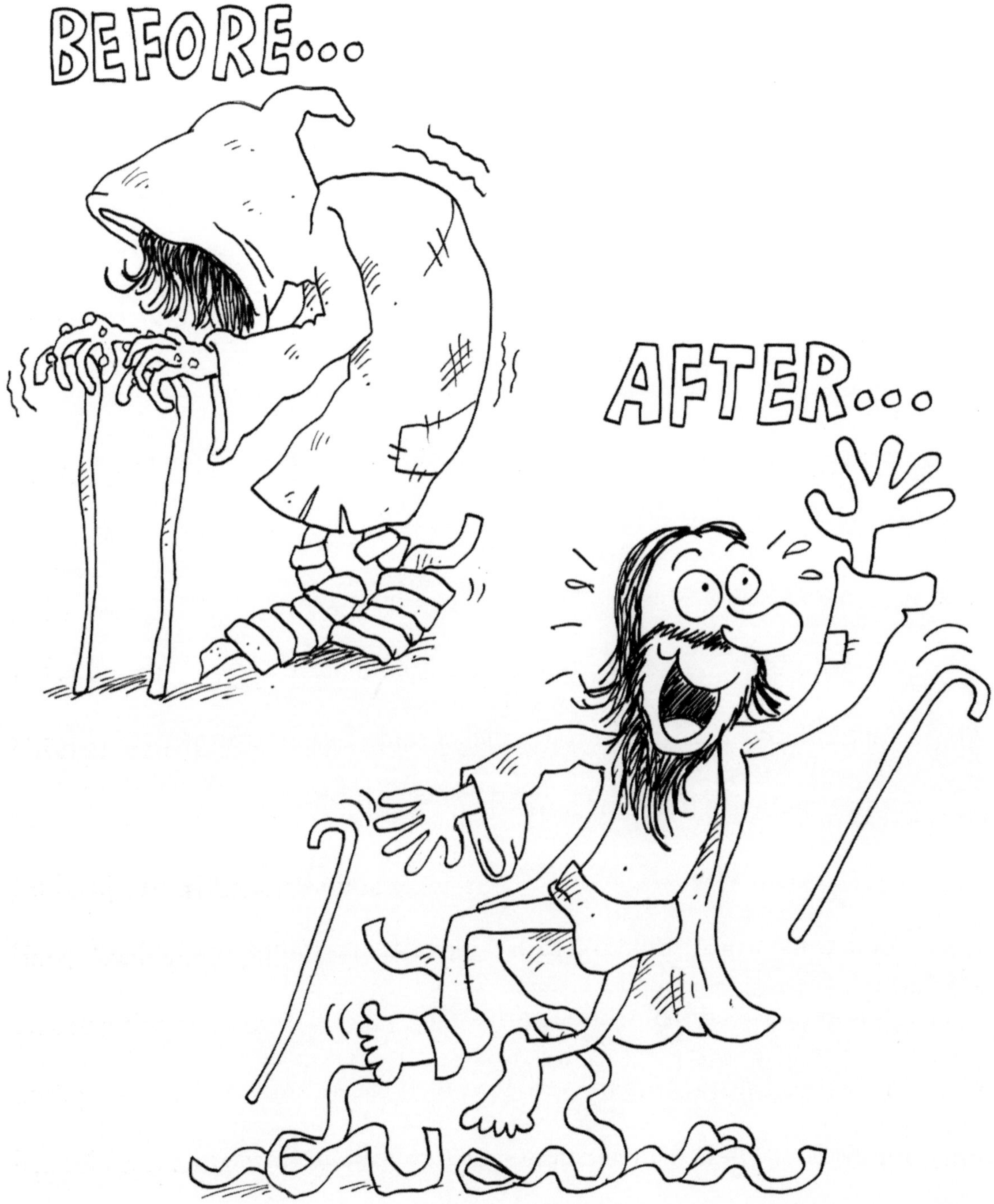
BEFORE...
AFTER...

One man remembers his manners

The tenth man, the Samaritan, ran his fingers over his face in silent wonder. Moments earlier, his skin had been as craggy as a walnut, and now it was smooth, soft and supple. His whole body was the same: like his nine companions, he was no longer a leper. He had been completely healed. He turned to look at Jesus: '**THANK YOU! PRAISE THE LORD!**' he shouted. Then he ran back, yelling breathlessly, '**GLORY TO GOD! GLORY TO GOD! GLORY TO GOD!**' As he flopped on his face at Jesus' feet, he breathed, '**HALLELUJAH!**'

Jesus looked down at this outsider – this foreigner – this Samaritan who, as every Jew knew, was rotten, revolting and wrong about religion. He smiled at him. Then he looked up and saw the nine Jewish men who were now fighting fit. They were laughing and patting each other on the back as they raced off to find their friends in the village. Jesus frowned and said loudly, 'Didn't I just heal ten of you? Where are the other nine? Aren't you even going to say thank you?' (The other nine were too busy cheering to hear him.) 'Isn't anyone going to give glory to God except this outsider?' (The other nine were congratulating each other on their amazing recovery – God didn't get a look-in.) Then Jesus looked down at the Samaritan, who was still lying at his feet like a faithful dog. He reached out, took the Samaritan's hands and helped him up. 'On your feet,' he said. 'It's time to get going.' Jesus looked into the Samaritan's eyes and smiled. 'Your faith has made you better.'

Dazed and delighted, the Samaritan walked towards the village. Jesus had healed him, and he knew in his heart that he wasn't unclean or unwelcome any more.

Jesus' friends wanted him to keep clear of lepers, and they weren't keen for him to mix with Samaritans, either. But Jesus went ahead and healed them all anyway, showing that God loves unclean, unwelcome people too. A lot of Jesus' Jewish followers wanted to keep God all for themselves, but stories like this show that God's love belongs to everyone – no one is left outside. Many of Jesus' own people – especially the good, religious ones – were shocked and offended by this. Read on for more stories of outrageous outsiders . . .

You can read the story of the ten lepers in Luke 17:11-19.

GREEDY MONEY-GRABBERS
Jesus welcomes tax collectors

An unlikely disciple

'That's three denarii you owe me,' said Levi, the richly dressed tax collector, sitting at his polished table behind his piles of cash.

'Three?!' exclaimed the grubby shepherd in front of him. 'That's three days' wages!'

'Not my fault,' sighed Levi. 'You didn't pay last time, and Roman rules are Roman rules – taxes have got to be paid.' The shepherd looked as if he were about to cry. He held out a grubby fist with his three hard-earned coins. Levi took them and made a mark on his list. Then he added two coins to the pile of cash on his left (*Two for the Romans*, he thought) and popped the other coin onto the pile on his right (*And one for me*).

The shepherd stomped out of the tax office muttering, 'It's a rip-off! That robber loves the Romans more than his own people!' As he walked into the crowded street, he bumped into Jesus, who was heading straight for Levi's office. The shepherd saw where he was going and snarled, 'Steer clear, mate. All tax collectors are traitors and thieves!'

Jesus stood in Levi's doorway and looked at the well-dressed man in front of him, with his piles of other people's cash. 'Follow me,' he said. Levi, who was also called Matthew, stopped counting his cash and stood up. Then – with no why, if or but – he followed Jesus. Just like that.

That night Jesus and his disciples had dinner at Levi's house. Levi's only friends were tax collectors, so the house was full of them. A dinner party full of traitors and thieves! People were shocked to see Jesus there. The men who worked for the Pharisees (those proud protectors of the Jewish religion) were watching the so-called Messiah. They tut-tutted and asked the disciples, 'What does he think he's doing?! Just look at him – eating with *tax collectors*!' They spat the words out as if they left a bad taste in their mouths.

Jesus heard them and, with his mouth full of bread, he said, 'Don't you get it? I'm not here for good people, but for sinners like these! Healthy people don't need a doctor, do they? But sick people do!' The Pharisees' men, who liked to think that they were very good people indeed, went off in a huff to report this rudeness.

The unexpected guest

Another day, another town . . . On this particular day, the streets of Jericho were packed, as if for a film premiere or a royal visit. The word had gone out – 'JESUS IS COMING!' – and now everyone wanted to catch a glimpse of the famous man. People stood ten deep along the road and trod on each other's toes. Children shoved to the front to get a better view.

One man who couldn't see anything except the back of other people's heads was Zacchaeus. He was dressed in fine robes and his hair was expensively oiled. Being the chief tax collector in the town, he was ridiculously rich, but everyone hated him because he ripped off the poor and creamed off the profits from his employees. Even the other tax collectors couldn't stand him.

Zacchaeus was a very short man and he was keen to see what Jesus looked like. However, when the shout went up, – '**HE'S HERE!**' – no one made way for him in the crowd, so he forgot his dignity and his fine clothes and climbed the nearest tree.

Men in the crowd pointed and laughed, '**HA HA!** Look at the money-grabbing monkey!'

From his high branch, Zacchaeus could see a knot of people moving slowly down the main street through the crowds. He spotted a man in the middle and thought he must be Jesus, and he watched as the famous teacher came closer. When Jesus was directly underneath his tree, Zacchaeus could see how tightly the crowds were pressing and how eagerly people were reaching out to touch their hero. Everyone wanted his attention. Suddenly, Jesus threw back his head and looked up into the tree. He stared straight at the tiny tax collector. '**HEY, ZACCHAEUS!**' yelled Jesus.

Then *everyone* looked up into the tree. Zacchaeus felt as if every unfriendly eye in Jericho was on him – it was like being pricked by a thousand pins.

'Jesus knows his name!' whispered one woman. 'I'll bet he knows all about his greedy money-grabbing!'

'Jesus knows a sinner when he sees one!' murmured her friend.

Now he's for it, thought everyone in Jericho with satisfaction, as they waited for Jesus to tell Zacchaeus off.

'**QUICK! GET DOWN HERE, ZACCHAEUS!**' shouted Jesus. '**I'VE GOT TO HAVE DINNER AT YOUR HOUSE TONIGHT!**'

The crowd gasped. This was *not* what they wanted to hear.

Zacchaeus couldn't believe it. He bumped and slithered down the tree and gabbled, 'Of course! I'd be delighted to welcome you!'

An unhappy grumble spread through the crowd like a bad cold. 'Why is Jesus going to be a guest in *that sinner's* house?' people complained. Many felt that they deserved the honour far more than the money-grabbing midget.

Zacchaeus knew what people were saying about him. He took a deep breath and, standing there in front of Jesus, he said loudly, '**LOOK, LORD! I'M GOING TO GIVE HALF OF WHAT I OWN TO THE POOR!**' The beggars on the street cheered loudly at this. He continued, '**AND IF I'VE CHEATED ANYONE**

OF ANYTHING, I'LL PAY THEM BACK FOUR TIMES WHAT I TOOK!' Everyone in the crowd started doing mental maths and counted back through all the years that Zacchaeus had been taking their taxes. Four times what he'd taken would be a fortune!

'**HOOOOORAAAAAY!**' they cheered.

Man on a mission

Jesus said to the crowd, 'Today this man has been saved, because he belongs to God, too.' Then he spelt out his mission so that everyone would understand what he was up to: 'You see, the Son of God has come to look for the lost and to save sinners.'

So Levi the taxman became Matthew the disciple, and Zacchaeus the chief tax collector changed his ways. Once again, Jesus showed that he was interested in unwelcome outsiders. His mission was not to have cosy chats with the powerful religious people in Jerusalem: he was going to spend his time with sinners and show them how to leave their bad ways behind. The powerful religious people were not pleased . . .

You can read the stories of Matthew and Zacchaeus in Mark 2:13-17 and Luke 19:1-10.

ENEMY INVADERS

Jesus helps a Roman centurion

The riot police

The town of Capernaum was full of Jesus' fans. Everywhere he went, crowds crushed him and desperate people begged him for help.

'Lord! Get rid of my leprosy!' one cried.

'My mother's got a fever!' shouted another.

'My son's got a demon!' yelled a third.

The noise was enormous and the excited crowds pushed and shoved in the narrow streets. The Roman soldiers on duty grabbed their helmets. Capernaum was their town (or it was now, since they had invaded the whole country – finders keepers) and they were always ready to act as riot police. They weren't keen on excited crowds. They kept the people in their place and they'd do whatever it took to keep the peace. Right now, they had their eye on Jesus and his troublesome followers.

'LOOK OUT! ROMANS!' shouted someone in the crowd. The disciples looked round to see the soldiers on the street standing to attention as a very big Roman in full armour headed towards Jesus like a charging bull. They recognised him as the local centurion. Usually he was kind to the Jews, but today he looked desperate. What was going on? Did he have orders to arrest Jesus for causing a riot?

The centurion barged through the crowd and stood in front of Jesus, panting. '**HELP, LORD!**' he blurted out. 'My servant is crippled! He's in bed at home in a terrible state! I think he's going to **DIE!**'

Jesus looked up at the massive Roman's red face. He didn't have to think twice. 'I'll come and cure him,' he said.

The centurion's jaw dropped. 'Lord, I don't deserve a home visit from you! But – look – just give the order and my servant will be healed. It's like the Roman army – I get my orders from the chaps in charge, and I tell my men what to do. When I say, "By the left – quick **MARCH!**" they march, and when I say, "About **TURN!**" they turn around.' (At this, the soldiers on the street leapt to their feet and did as they were told.) 'If I give my slave an order – "**DO IT!**" – he does it straight away. So if you give a direct order, Sir, I know my servant will get better.'

Jesus stared at the centurion in amazement. He was so *sure*! Jesus exclaimed loudly to all the people around him, '**THIS GUY REALLY GETS IT!** He's got more faith than any of my Jewish followers! He knows that God is the Boss!'

The Jewish followers in the crowd looked at their feet and shuffled. They all wished Jesus had picked on them to praise their faith. The centurion looked pleased and a bit sheepish. Some of the followers muttered, 'Teacher's pet!'

But Jesus hadn't finished. '**LISTEN**! I'm telling you that people like this Roman will come from all over the world to God's great big party in heaven. *They* will be feasting with Abraham, while Abraham's family* – all you sons and daughters of Israel – will be thrown out into the Deep Dark. *You* will be weeping and wailing and gnashing your teeth in despair!' Jesus' Jewish followers were horrified: they were God's special people! How could they be left out of heaven while this Roman got in?

Jesus turned to the centurion. 'Go – you'll get everything your faith deserves.'

The instant miracle

At that very moment, back in the centurion's house, the paralysed servant woke up. His mind cleared like the sky after a terrible storm and he suddenly realised that *nothing hurt any more*. He took a deep breath. Now there was a tingle in his toes . . . now there was a fizzing in his fingers . . . now there was a tickling and a buzzing and a quivering running all through his body like electricity. He

* God promised that all Abraham's descendants would be his special people. You can read about his promise in *The crucial cut* in **Beastly Bible Stories 2**.

could move his legs! He could lift his arms! HE COULD STAND UP! He leapt off the bed and stretched. Then he began to dance . . . He was still jigging for joy when his boss, the centurion, burst through the door. The master and the slave looked at each other with silly grins on their faces. Then, in spite of all the rules about who was in charge, the centurion gave his favourite servant a great big hug.

In Jesus' time, the Roman Empire was the world's biggest superpower. Jesus and all his followers lived under Roman rule and people hated the enemy invaders who had taken over their country. Many Jews hoped that Jesus would be a battle-winning hero who would defeat the Romans and take back their land. You can imagine how upset they were when Jesus helped a Roman centurion instead! Jesus promised that people from all over the world would be able to join in God's great big party in heaven, and that's good news for us. It means that God doesn't have favourites — everyone can get close to him.

You can read the story of the centurion and his servant in Matthew 8:5-13 and Luke 7:1-10.

THE SPECIAL SISTERS
Martha and Mary

Jesus drops in for dinner

Jesus was very thirsty and his feet hurt. He and his crowd of followers had been walking all day in the desert hills near Jerusalem and now their sandals were dusty, their throats were dry and their bellies were empty. Just then, they saw a milestone for Bethany village, and that gave Jesus a good idea. 'Hey,' he said, and everyone stopped to listen. 'How about we pop over to Bethany and drop in on Lazarus, Martha and Mary?'*

'But, Lord, they're not expecting us,' said Philip.

'Oh, they won't mind!' replied Jesus, breezily. 'They're always happy to have visitors!'

And so they were. Lazarus was out, but Mary and Martha were thrilled to see Jesus – he was their best friend. Both sisters hugged him hard, but as Martha did so she was writing a list of jobs in her head. She was the elder sister – the hostess – and today was going to be hard work. It was wonderful to see Jesus, of

---

* You can read more about them in the dramatic story *Dead man walking* in **Beastly Bible Stories 5**.

course, but he always brought heaps of followers with him. So many unexpected guests! This was Martha's list of jobs:

TO DO (Martha)

1. Wash guests' feet (need to fetch more water first)
2. Serve drinks
3. Check ingredients and decide what everyone is going to eat for dinner (for 16 at least!)
4. Prepare and serve snacks to keep everyone going (Nuts? Olives? Have we got enough?)
5. Make dinner (Will there be enough bread?)
6. Serve dinner to guests
7. Eat dinner (Have we got space for everyone to sit down?)
8. Clear dishes and wash up

Mary preferred to think about one thing at a time. If she had been the sort of person who makes lists of jobs – and she wasn't – her list would have been very short:

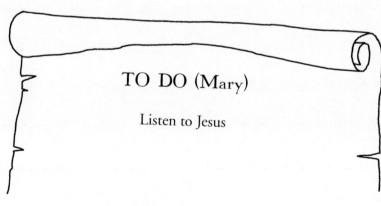

TO DO (Mary)

Listen to Jesus

An unpopular choice

The sisters welcomed their guests into their home. All the men sat down around Jesus to hear what he had to say. He started to tell another story – one of those stories of his that seemed to be about quite ordinary things, but was actually about something else – and Mary did what she wanted to do most in the world: she sat down with the men and listened to Jesus. Some of the disciples stared and others tut-tutted at her. *Doesn't she know the rules?* one thought.

You see, women in Jesus' time weren't allowed to learn about God with men. They were kept separate in the synagogues. *This sort of high-level religious instruction is men's business,* thought another disapproving disciple. However, no one dared to object out loud, and Jesus simply carried on talking while Mary carried on listening.

Martha tried to listen, too, but what with ordering the servant to fetch more water and counting jars of pickled fish and checking that the cheese hadn't gone off and shelling the nuts and hunting for more honey and baking extra bread, she got distracted. The harder she worked, the hotter and crosser she became. There was so much to do!

Martha could hear the rise and fall of Jesus' voice in the next room, and the murmurs and laughter from his adoring audience of disciples. And Mary.

That useless sister of mine! thought Martha angrily. *Why on earth isn't she out here helping me?* Martha stomped about in the kitchen and crashed and banged the dishes, hoping Mary would take the hint and give her a hand – but no.

Finally Martha lost her temper and forgot her manners: she burst into the next room, interrupted Jesus and blurted out, 'LORD! DON'T YOU CARE THAT MY SISTER HAS LEFT ME TO SLAVE AWAY ALL BY MYSELF?' Everyone looked at their feet in awkward silence. What a way to speak to Jesus! But there was no stopping Martha now – she actually ordered Jesus about like a kitchen servant! 'So TELL MY SISTER to come and HELP ME!' The disciples stared at Martha. Some of them glared at Mary because they thought her sister had a point. *Doesn't Mary know that a woman's place is in the kitchen?* they thought.

But Jesus thought differently. He looked at the fierce woman in front of him and smiled – a real, crinkly-around-the-eyes smile. 'Martha, Martha,' he said, 'you're worried and stressed out because you've got so much to do. But there's only one thing that really needs doing. Your sister has made the right choice, and nobody is going to take that away from her.'

If you were Martha, what would you do? Would you:

a. Sit down with Mary and listen to Jesus?
b. Stomp back into the kitchen in an even worse mood?
c. Tell the disciples to get their own dinner?

The Bible doesn't tell us what Martha did next! We'll just have to imagine the end of the story for ourselves. Do you think anyone got any dinner that night?

EXTRA SMELLY STORY – HEAVEN'S SCENT

You have already read the story of when Lazarus died and Jesus miraculously brought him back from the dead. There is one more story about Martha and Mary from Bethany village.

This dinner party had been planned and properly prepared for. Jesus was the guest of honour at the home of Martha, Mary and Lazarus, because the sisters wanted to thank him for his amazing miracle that had brought their brother back to life. Once again, Jesus arrived with heaps of followers, but this time there were extra onlookers: crowds of locals had come to gawp at Jesus the miracle-maker and goggle at Lazarus the ex-corpse.

Jesus and his friends lay down comfortably around a low table and Martha served up the finest feast she could afford – nothing but the best for Jesus. With her own hands she had salted the meat, baked the bread, toasted the almonds, spiced the olives, honeyed the figs, chopped the dates and picked the pomegranates. Mary had prepared one special thing for Jesus – and it was a secret.

At the feast, Jesus and Lazarus tucked in. Lazarus felt that food tasted better than ever since he'd got a second chance at living, and Jesus knew that he didn't have much time left – there wouldn't be many more dinners like this to enjoy.*

After dinner, Mary fetched her secret surprise. It was heavy – it weighed half a kilo – and very, very expensive. The secret was hidden inside a stone jar which was a cool, creamy white, like the moon. Mary carried the jar carefully to Jesus and knelt down at his feet. Then she did something that made the disciples and onlookers gasp in shock: she took off her head-covering and let loose all her long, dark hair! This may not sound like a big deal to you, but in those days it was almost as bad as taking off your clothes in public. Only a woman's husband was supposed to see her bare head. Mary looked up at Jesus and held the moony jar in both hands. Then she tapped it sharply on the floor and – **CRACK** – the sealed top broke off and – **SLUURP, SLOOOP** – out poured great globs of thick, golden oil.

PHHHHOOOOOOOOOOOFFFFFFFFF! A beautiful smell exploded in the room, like a bomb made of blossom. It wasn't just perfume: this precious oil had a deep, strong smell, like flowers and honey and incense all rolled into one. It was called *nard*. Mary scooped it up in her hands – it was running all over the place like liquid gold – and began to rub it into Jesus' feet with her hands and hair. As the oil warmed on his skin, the scent

* Less than a week later, Jesus would be killed. He knew what was going to happen to him. You can read all about it in *Extraordinary Easter* in **Beastly Bible Stories 7**.

bloomed like a giant lily opening in the sun. For a moment, time seemed to stand still: the astonishing perfume filled everyone's nostrils and lungs. A perfume cloud enveloped the whole house.

But Judas, one of Jesus' disciples, interrupted. '**HEY!**' he shouted, as he watched the precious perfume oil running between Jesus' toes and onto the dusty floor. '**WHY DIDN'T ANYONE SELL THIS PERFUME?! IT'S WORTH NEARLY A YEAR'S WAGES! WE COULD HAVE GIVEN THAT MONEY TO THE POOR!**' (You might think that makes him sound caring but in fact, his job was to look after all the disciples' money, and he often stole it. Judas wouldn't have given the perfume money to the poor – he would have pocketed it.)

'Leave her alone,' replied Jesus. 'She bought this oil for when I'm in my grave.* You'll always have the poor – but you won't always have me!'

The house smelled of nard for weeks, and so did Mary's hair. Everyone who was there that night took the scent home with them in their clothes. The next day, when Jesus rode into Jerusalem on a donkey, he still smelled as rich as a king. Just a few days after that, as he was beaten and battered and killed, the lingering perfume reminded Jesus of the friends who loved him.

---

* People used to rub perfume oil such as nard or myrrh onto dead bodies before they were buried.

Jesus always welcomed women. He treated them as human beings and ignored the rules that said what women weren't allowed to do. He encouraged the special sisters, Martha and Mary, to learn alongside the men, and he gladly accepted Mary's special gift. In another Bible story, it was a woman (and a Samaritan woman, too!) to whom Jesus first said the amazing words, 'I AM the Messiah.'* Watch out for the way Jesus welcomes women throughout **The Terrific New Testament***.*

You can read these stories about Martha and Mary in Luke 10:38-42 and John 12:1-11.

* John 4:1-42.

KIDS WELCOME!
Jesus and children

Grumpy grown-ups

Jesus was on the road again, preaching and teaching all over Judea. Crowds of fans and followers trailed him wherever he went, and the Pharisees (those proud protectors of the Jewish religion) stalked him and tested his teaching. Everyone had a question for Jesus:

'What does Moses say about marriage?' asked the Pharisees.

'Can you make me better?' cried a blind man.

'Which one of us do you like best?' asked the disciples, missing the point as usual.

'How do I get into God's kingdom?' asked a good man. Everyone wanted to know the answer to that one, because God's kingdom sounded wonderful. To some, it seemed like heaven – a perfect Promised Land where you could live happily ever after. To others, it was the opposite of the Roman Empire: kind, fair and good, God's kingdom was ruled by God and everything would be done his way. People hoped this kingdom would come any day now. One thing was for sure: God's kingdom was like a wonderful party and everyone wanted an invitation.

However, before Jesus could say a word about the kingdom, a little kid came up and grabbed his hand. Then a mum held out her baby for Jesus to cuddle. Soon there was a stampede of small, dirty feet as every kid in the crowd decided that *they* wanted to get close to Jesus, too. They were fed up with being stuck behind tall grown-ups and not being able to see what was going on. The disciples watched the grubby children toddling and racing towards Jesus, then they stepped in like security guards. '**STAND BACK!**' shouted Peter.

The children ignored him and cried, '**ME FIRST! ME FIRST!**' as they pushed towards Jesus.

'**PARENTS!** Please control your children!' ordered James.

'This is **NO PLACE FOR LITTLE ONES** – the rest of us are trying to **LISTEN!**' yelled Matthew.

'Leave the Saviour alone – he's busy! **SHOO!**' hissed John.

'**SHUT UP!**' shouted Jesus. The children jumped. For a moment, they thought he was talking to them – but he wasn't. He was glaring at the disciples who, once again, had got it wrong. The disciples went bright red and looked awkward, like pushy prefects who were about to be told off by the head teacher. 'Let the kids come to me,' said Jesus, firmly. '**DON'T STOP THEM.**'

Kids' kingdom

'**YAAAAAAAY!**' cheered the children. They pushed past the disciples and ran to Jesus. When they found themselves at his feet, they felt suddenly shy and wondered what to do next. Jesus looked down at the children around him – tall kids, skinny kids, fat kids, kids with runny noses, kids with dirty feet, kids with scabby knees, kids who couldn't stand still for a minute, kids who didn't know what to say, kids who were all grinning at him – and he said to the grown-ups, 'See this? This is what God's kingdom looks like!'

The grown-ups were shocked. 'But those children will make a mess! And they don't know how to behave!' one hissed.

'They're just children – what do *they* know about God?' another muttered.

'Who is *he* to tell us what God's kingdom is like?' wondered the Pharisees.

Jesus ignored the muttering and said to everyone, 'God is inviting **ALL OF YOU** to his kingdom!' With that, he opened his arms to the children and grinned. They forgot their shyness and threw themselves at Jesus. They hugged his legs, climbed on his back and squeezed their arms around his neck. Jesus laughed as he nearly toppled over with children climbing all over him like monkeys in a tree. He said to the grown-ups, 'If you don't accept God's invitation like this – **OOF!**' – he caught his breath as a big kid gave him a huge, happy bear hug – 'then you'll never get into his kingdom at all!'

The disciples looked at their feet and the Pharisees tutted disapprovingly as Jesus laid his hands on every child's head and blessed them. The children walked tall as they headed back into the crowd: they felt like princes and princesses in God's kingdom.

In Jesus' time, children didn't have human rights as they do today, and they didn't have any public importance. Still today, Jewish children become adults at the age of 12 (for girls) and 13 (for boys). Only then can they play a full part in Jewish religious and community life. So it was very unusual for an important religious teacher like Jesus to single out little kids as being extra-specially important.

You can read the story of Jesus and the children in Mark 10:13-16.

THE UNTOUCHABLE WOMAN AND THE DYING DAUGHTER

A double miracle

A desperate dad and an unwelcome woman

The crowds around Jesus were bigger and noisier than ever. Wherever he went, he was mobbed by fans and followers. In this particular crowd, two people were especially keen to get close. One was an important man – Jairus, the leader of the local synagogue. People moved respectfully out of his way as he headed straight for Jesus and made his bold request: 'Lord! Please come to my house and save my daughter! She's at death's door!'

The other person who was desperate to see Jesus was a woman whom people tried not to notice, because she had a disease. She had been bleeding non-stop for years. She had tried every doctor she could afford. None of them had made her any better, and many had made her worse. She had heard about Jesus' healing miracles and hardly dared to hope that he might be able to help her. She crept through the crowds, trying not to get in anyone's way. She could

45

just see the back of Jesus' head. She thought to herself, *If I can touch him – even if it's just his clothes – I'll be saved.* She ducked down between people's feet and, trying not to get stepped on, she reached out her hand and managed to touch the hem of Jesus' robe. Immediately she felt the difference inside her – it was as if someone had turned off a tap. Her bleeding had stopped!

At that very moment, Jesus said loudly, 'Who touched me?'

His disciples looked at the pushing, pawing crowds on all sides and snapped, '*Really?* "Who touched me?" You're in the middle of a mob like this and you're asking *that*? **EVERYONE'S** trying to get their hands on you!'

'This was different,' insisted Jesus. 'I felt the power going out of me.' He didn't say another word but scanned the faces of the crowd for the woman he knew had touched him.

Knowing that he was looking for her, the woman made her way towards him. She was shaking with fear as she fell at his feet and told him everything that had happened to her. 'It was me. I've been bleeding for 12 years. No doctor has been able to make me better.' At this, the crowds drew back in horror. People shuddered. *Yuck!* they thought. Touching a woman with a problem like that would make them unclean.* The poor woman was used to this reaction – no one had wanted to go near her for years. But Jesus didn't flinch. The woman continued, 'You

---

* You can read about the strict Jewish rules for keeping clean in *Clean and unclean* in **Beastly Bible Stories 2**. There were special rules about blood.

were my last hope, and when I touched you, my bleeding stopped!'

Jesus smiled broadly and said, 'Daughter, your faith has saved you – go in peace and be well again.'

'**HOOOORAAAAYY!**' The crowds cheered wildly at this miracle, but Jairus, the leader of the synagogue, didn't cheer. He was still worried sick about his dying daughter. Jesus had already been delayed – would he be in time for another miracle? As if overhearing these anxious thoughts, Jesus turned to him and said, 'Come on, Jairus, let's go and see your little girl.'

'Lord, she's the only daughter I've got – she's just 12 years old,' said Jairus. 'I only hope we're not too late.' There was a bustling at the back of the crowd. He'd barely finished speaking when a man barged through and blurted out, 'Your daughter is dead – why bother the teacher any more?'

Jesus saw Jairus stand stock still, frozen with fear at the terrible thing he had to face. Jesus put his hand on his arm and said, '**DON'T BE FRIGHTENED – only BELIEVE**.' Then Jesus turned to the expectant disciples and the over-excited crowds and said, 'Peter – James – John – come with me. The rest of you – stay here.'

'**AAAAAAWWWWW!**' moaned the crowd, disappointed that they weren't going to be in on the action any more. The rest of the disciples felt rather left out, too.

47

Rise and shine!

At the synagogue leader's house everyone was crying, because in Jesus' time, family, friends and neighbours all mourned together, and the bigger the grief, the louder the wailing. Jesus walked straight in and shouted above the noise, **'WHY ARE YOU LOT MAKING SUCH A RACKET?** Why all these tears? The little girl isn't dead – she's just asleep!'

The mourners were not impressed. 'Huh! Not dead? A likely story!'

'Asleep? As if! She hasn't got a pulse!'

'What does *he* know? She took her last breath ages ago!'

'GET OUT! ALL OF YOU!' shouted Jesus. Like a bouncer in a night club, he threw them all out and slammed the door in their faces.

Jesus gathered up the small group that remained – the girl's parents, Peter, James and John – and led them to where the girl's still body lay. Jesus knelt down beside her and held her small, cold hand. He spoke to her in Aramaic, the first language they had both learned to speak as children: '*Talitha Koum.*' This means, 'Little girl, it's time to get up!' It was the same thing her mum said to her every morning, but this time it was Jesus speaking, in a voice that was both gentler than a lullaby and louder than thunder.

Everyone waited, hardly daring to breathe. Suddenly – **'HUUUHHHH!'** – someone *did* breathe, very deeply indeed – and it was the little girl! Her eyes

opened and she saw Jesus sitting beside her. He smiled at her – a real, crinkly-around-the-eyes smile. He squeezed her warm hand. Then, just as she did every morning, the little girl jumped straight out of bed, wide awake and ready for the day.

And then – what a hullabaloo! The girl hugged her mum and dad, the disciples hugged each other and everyone hugged Jesus. They all chattered excitedly at once:

'It's **AMAZING!** Did you – '

'How can she – '

'It's a **MIRACLE!** I've never – '

'I know! It's **WONDERFUL!** Who would – '

'Praise the – '

'**LORD!** How can we ever thank – '

'**WHAT YOU NEED TO DO NOW**,' said Jesus, firmly interrupting the excited babble, '**IS GIVE THIS GIRL SOMETHING TO EAT**. I'll bet she's hungry!'

The little girl nodded and grinned. While her parents fell over each other to find her a feast, Jesus said to everyone in the room, 'Don't tell anyone what happened here today. **OK?**'

Everyone nodded – thinking of just one person they might tell, if they promised to keep it a secret. And so the secret was shared until the whole town heard it, one person at a time.

In Jesus' time, neither women nor children were believed to be as important as men, but these stories show how happy Jesus was to help both women and children, and how much he valued them. This double miracle also reminds us that Jesus didn't always follow the rules of his own religion: it was important for religious leaders to remain clean, and touching a dead body or someone who was bleeding would make them very unclean – but Jesus didn't care. For him, making the woman better and bringing the little girl back to life were far more important.

Read on to see Jesus the troublemaking teacher break more rules . . .

You can read about this double miracle in Mark 5:21-43 and Luke 8:40-56.

GO AWAY!

Jesus faces the devil and his neighbours

A long way down

Jesus stood on the edge of the cliff and looked down at the drop. His stomach lurched. A loose stone slipped off and plunged straight down the cliff face: it bounced off the grey, weather-beaten slab and rattled down a steep slope of slippery scree; finally it fell onto the jagged rocks that were sticking up through the earth like broken bones through skin. Jesus swayed slightly.

'**DOWN YOU GO!**' yelled a voice. For the second time in less than a month, someone was urging Jesus to jump.

Jesus vs the devil

The first time it had happened, he'd just spent several long and lonely weeks in the wilderness – the place where the wild things are. Jesus had been hurried there by the Holy Spirit, who had pushed him forward like a personal trainer. You know what the wilderness was like for John the Baptiser* – well, it was the

* You can read about him in **Beastly Bible Stories 5**. In *Locusts, bees and a dead camel*, you can find out what life was like in the wilderness, and in *The Saviour gets a soaking* you can read what happened to Jesus immediately before this story.

same for Jesus: nothing but wind and sand, stones and bones for mile upon sun-scorched mile. The sun glared at him all day, then left him to freeze at night, with nothing but the scurryings and slitherings of unseen creatures for company. Jesus had left behind crowds of fans and a river full of fresh water to go into the wilderness, and he stayed there all alone for 40 fiery days and 40 freezing nights. He slept rough, drank little and ate nothing at all. Before long, he was so hungry he could have eaten a camel.

That was when the devil turned up. You've heard of the devil, of course – God's enemy who is bold, bad and dangerous to know. He's always trying to get one over on God. This time he'd come to have a go at Jesus. At first, he tried sounding sympathetic. 'Aah, poor you,' he said. 'You must be *starving*.'

Jesus stared at him and his tummy growled.

The devil picked up a big stone and continued, 'If you're *really* the Son of God, turn this stone into a loaf of bread. Go on, you know you want to.'

Jesus looked at the flat, round, brown stone in the devil's hand. It did look like one of his mum's home-made loaves . . . His mouth watered. Then he looked into the devil's cold eyes and answered him with words from the Bible: ' "Human beings don't just need bread to live." ' Both he and the devil knew what came next: ' "They need every word that comes from God's mouth, too." ' It was those very words of God that Jesus had come to share with people. He was a man on a mission.

VOOOOOOM! Straight away the devil conjured up a vision, using the sky like a 360-degree cinema screen. He showed Jesus a glittering display of all the great kingdoms of the world: there were grand palaces, cheering crowds, fabulous feasts and chests full of treasure. Jesus watched red carpets unrolling, servants bowing and soldiers marching to their king's command. The devil let Jesus take it all in, then he said slyly, 'I could give you all this, you know! It's all mine, and I can give it to anyone I want to. It will **ALL** be yours – if you worship me.'

Jesus stared at the thrones and crowns and piles of cash. Then he looked into the devil's smiling face and answered him with God's first and most important rule: '"Worship the Lord your God – only him; no one else."'*

WHOOOOOSH! Immediately the devil whisked Jesus to Jerusalem and placed him on the pinnacle of the Temple. Jesus teetered on the edge and looked down at the drop. His stomach lurched. A tiny pebble slipped off the roof and plunged straight down onto the pavement below.

'If you're *really* the Son of God,' said the devil, '**JUMP!**' Then God's enemy decided to try some words from the Bible: 'It says, "He will send angels to protect you," and "They will catch you, so you won't even stub your toe on a rock." Go on, *prove* that God is really looking after you – get him to send an

* You can read the rest of God's important rules in *Laws for living* in **Beastly Bible Stories 2**.

57

army of angels to rescue his Son!' He gave Jesus a little nudge. '**DOWN YOU GO***!*'

Jesus stared at the hard stone pavement stretching out far below him. He swayed slightly. Then he looked at the devil's determined expression and replied, 'It also says, "Do not test God." **GO AWAY, YOU DEVIL***!*'

PHWUMMPPP! Suddenly Jesus was back in the wilderness and the devil was nowhere to be seen. He had given up – for now . . .

Annoying the neighbours

Then Jesus headed out of the wilderness. He was full of the Holy Spirit's power, like a hot-air balloon ready for take-off. He was on a special mission and it was time to begin by healing, helping, preaching and teaching in the local villages. When he stood up to speak in the synagogues, all the locals were impressed.

'What a terrific sermon!' said one.

'Such wisdom!' said another.

'He's a wonderful teacher, whoever he is!' said a third. Wherever Jesus went, the crowds of fans and followers grew bigger.

All went well until Jesus came to his home town of Nazareth. He had grown up there, and all the locals knew his family, but were they proud of him? Were his old neighbours pleased to see him? Did they welcome him as a homecoming hero? Here's what happened . . .

Jesus did what he always did in the towns he visited: he went to preach in the synagogue on the Sabbath. He would read from the Scriptures and then give them a sermon. In Nazareth, he read from the prophet Isaiah,* who told God's people what their Saviour would say when he came:

"God's Holy Spirit is upon me, because he has chosen me to bring good news to the poor. He has sent me to bring release for prisoners and sight for the blind and freedom for everyone who is downtrodden."

Then Jesus rolled up the Scripture scroll and faced the crowded synagogue, ready to speak. Everyone settled down for a sermon about Isaiah's prophecy and the promised Saviour – but what Jesus had to say wouldn't take long: 'Today this prophecy has come true. Right here. Right now. I'm the One he has sent.'

There was a stunned silence: '   '

Then everyone started talking at once. '**WHAT** did he say?'

'Did he just say he's the **SAVIOUR?**'

'How can he be? He's Joseph the builder's boy!'

'His brothers and sisters are right here!'

* You can read about Isaiah's prophecies in *Death or glory* in **Beastly Bible Stories 1**.

'Where did all this come from, then?'

'**WHO DOES HE THINK HE IS?!**'

Over the racket, Jesus said, 'You're going to ask me to make miracles happen here, but no prophet is ever welcome at home. Even Elijah and Elisha,* those great prophets, didn't heal people in Israel. They helped the Syrians instead!'

At this mention of Israel's arch enemies, there was a roar of outrage. '**WHHHAAAAAT?!!** Is he going to help our enemies? How **DARE** he!' It was bad enough that a local boy should claim to be the Messiah, but to say he wasn't going to do any miracles for his own people – **WELL!**

All at once, respectful worshippers became rioters, and the congregation turned into an angry mob. '**THROW HIM OUT! THROW HIM OUT!**' they chanted. Furious locals surged around Jesus and shoved him out of the synagogue.

'**GO AWAY AND LEAVE US ALONE!**' someone yelled.

Then they decided that the front door wasn't far enough – they wanted him out of the town as well. '**CHUCK HIM OFF THE CLIFF!**' yelled a wild young man.

* You can read some of the stories about these prophets in *On fire* in **Beastly Bible Stories 1.**

A long way down

'**YAAAAAAY!**' cheered the crowds. Jesus was caught up in the crush as they headed for the high cliffs outside the town until, for the second time that month, Jesus found himself looking down at a sheer drop.

'**DOWN YOU GO!**' yelled a voice. Then an argument broke out in the crowd – should they really kill him? Did he deserve it? Wasn't he Joseph the builder's son, after all? As they argued amongst themselves, Jesus pulled his cloak over his head and ducked down in the middle of the mob. He wriggled out and was off down the hill before anyone realised he'd gone. He caught his breath, then headed straight for the next town. After all, he was a man on a mission, and he didn't have much time.

Christians remember Jesus' time in the wilderness every year. During Lent (the 40 days before Easter) many people give up eating meat, chocolate or something else to remind themselves of the 40 days Jesus spent being hungry and resisting temptation. Jesus' unwelcome return to his home town of Nazareth reminds us that he had enemies as well as fans and followers. This was only the beginning of his troublemaking teaching . . .

You can read these stories in Luke 4:1-30, Matthew 4:1-11 and Matthew 13:54-58.

THROWING STONES
Jesus stands up to a mob

A trick question and a trap
'STONE HER! STONE HER! STONE THE SINNER!'

yelled the mob. They picked up stones the size of big fists, chose the heaviest ones with the sharpest edges and took aim at the shaking woman who was still in her nightie. The day had hardly begun and she had been dragged out of bed by the scribes (the Scripture experts) and the Pharisees (those proud protectors of the Jewish religion). The case was clear:

> **Her crime:** she had broken number seven of the Ten Commandments: 'Be faithful in marriage.' The scribes and the Pharisees had found her with a man who wasn't her husband.

> **Her punishment:** to be stoned to death, just like the Law of Moses said.

The Pharisees had been keeping an eye on Jesus and they had seen how much he loved sinners. Some of his best friends were money-grabbing tax collectors!

He'd healed a Samaritan, who was wrong about religion! He'd even helped a rotten Roman! So now they planned to trap Jesus in public with a trick question. This was their plan:

The Pharisees would take the woman to Jesus and ask, 'Should we stone this sinner like Moses says?'

Jesus could say, 'Yes.'

Then the Pharisees would reply, 'Aha! You don't love sinners, after all! You're a **LIAR!**'

On the other hand, Jesus could say, 'No.'

Then the Pharisees would reply, 'So you're saying that Moses was **WRONG** – how dare you! You're a **TERRIBLE TEACHER!**' Either way, Jesus would be in the wrong and the Pharisees would win back his followers. That was the plan: how could it possibly fail?

Jesus outwits everyone

So the Pharisees ordered their guards to drag the quaking woman to the Temple, followed by the scribes and the mob with sharp stones. Jesus was sitting on the steps in the shade and teaching. Although it was still early in the morning, a huge crowd had gathered to hear him. The Pharisees pushed through the crowd and presented the woman to him as if they were cats dropping a

doomed mouse. The woman saw hands reaching down all around her to grab rocks and stones.

'**STONE HER! STONE HER! STONE THE SINNER!**' yelled the mob again.

The Pharisees said to Jesus, 'Teacher, we found this woman breaking Commandment Number Seven! In the Law, Moses says she should be stoned to death. What do you say? Should we stone this sinner?' The scribes and the Pharisees held their breath. Would he answer 'Yes' or 'No'?

Jesus didn't bother to stand up when the Pharisees spoke to him. He stayed sitting on the steps and said nothing. Everyone waited. Then he began writing (or was he drawing?) with his finger on the dusty steps. Everyone watched.

What's he doing? wondered the Pharisees.

'Ahem,' coughed a scribe. The silence was getting awkward.

'**WELL?**' demanded a Pharisee eventually. 'What's your answer?'

At last Jesus stood up. 'Mr Perfect can throw the first stone at her. If you've never done a single thing wrong in your life, you can start the stoning. Be my guest.' Then he sat down again and doodled in the dust.

That's it? thought the Pharisees. *But he didn't say 'Yes' or 'No'!* They looked at each other and whispered, 'What do we do now?'

Jesus ignored them and carried on doodling as if to say, *You heard.*

They had heard, all right. The older and wiser Pharisees were the first to realise that their plan had backfired: Jesus had trapped *them*. No one could honestly say that he was perfect! One by one they dropped their stones and walked away, shaking their heads. The scribes followed them. Some of the younger, more bloodthirsty members of the mob tried to find a way around Jesus' words so they could hurl rocks at the woman's head after all – but they couldn't.

A new life

The trembling woman heard scores of stones thud harmlessly to the ground and saw many pairs of dusty feet shuffling away. Finally she dared to look up, and she saw nobody there except herself and Jesus. He smiled at her and asked, 'Where have they gone? Hasn't anyone condemned you?'

The woman gulped. For the first time since her arrest, someone was inviting her to speak for herself. She said shyly, 'No one, Lord.'

Jesus looked into her eyes and said gently but firmly, 'Then I don't condemn you, either. Now off you go – and don't sin any more.'

The woman nodded. That was a promise she meant to keep. Then, like a mouse that has been unexpectedly rescued from a cat's claws, she scurried away.

*Jesus is the only person in this story who **is** perfect – and he's the only one who doesn't condemn the woman or want to punish her. However, he doesn't let her off the hook, either, because when he tells her to go he also orders her to stop doing wrong. This story shows God's forgiveness in action: he doesn't want us to do bad things, but he is always ready to forgive us when we do and to let us have a second chance.*

You can read this story in John 8:1-11.

'LOVE YOUR ENEMIES!'
Jesus' hard lessons

The dodgy dozen

It was time for Jesus to pick his team of disciples. He had loads of followers to choose from, so he asked for God's help. Jesus spent a whole night praying on his own in the mountains, and early the next morning he was ready to make his final selection. Here's the line-up:

1. Simon the fisherman (Jesus calls him Peter)

2. Andrew the fisherman, Simon's brother

3. James the fisherman

4. John the fisherman, James' brother (Jesus nicknamed this pair 'the Thunder Boys' because of their stormy tempers!)

5. Philip (he was the one who counted heads and worked out costs at the all-you-can-eat picnic*)

6. Bartholemew (also known as Nathanael)

7. Matthew (also known as Levi. He used to be an unpopular tax collector**)

* In **Beastly Bible Stories 5**.
** You met him in *Greedy money-grabbers* earlier in this book.

8. Thomas (he doesn't always accept what everyone tells him*)

9. James, Alphaeus' son (we don't know much about him)

10. Simon (Jesus nicknamed him 'the Zealot', either because he was very keen (zealous) or because he'd been a member of the fierce anti-Roman gang, the Zealots)

11. Thaddeus (also known as Judas, James' son. We don't know much about him, either)

12. Judas Iscariot (don't trust him – he gets up to no good later on**)

So Jesus picked this unpredictable bunch of local lads. They had plenty of fishing experience between them but none of them had been trained to preach or teach. Some had bad tempers, some had a past they'd rather forget and some were not to be trusted – not so much a dream team as a dodgy dozen! Nevertheless, Jesus chose them to be his special squad of disciples, also known as the apostles.

Good news – hooray!

Jesus led his team down the mountain to the flatlands where the crowds were waiting for them. These crowds were bigger and noisier than ever: there were locals from Jerusalem and all over Judea, and people had travelled from the distant seaside towns just to see Jesus. When the disciples reached the foot of

* He's the star of *Holey Lord* in **Beastly Bible Stories 8**.
** He has an important part to play in *Extraordinary Easter* in **Beastly Bible Stories 7**.

the mountain they saw a heaving, multicoloured sea of people surging in their direction.

'**JESUS IS COMING!**' yelled the fans who spotted him first. A wave of people swept forwards and their arms stretched out like hundreds of jellyfish tentacles. The disciples tried not to cringe as hands covered with boils and sticky bandages reached past them to grab Jesus. They gawped as they saw the fingers touch Jesus' tunic – the boils melted away and left nothing but clean, healthy skin! Jesus turned to the left and to the right, touching hands and faces all around him. **SWOOSH!** He wiped out one man's leprosy. **CRAICK!** He clicked a woman's broken leg back into place. **WHOOSH!** He banished bad spirits. Miracle after miracle! The crowds went wild.

Then Jesus looked at his disciples and started to speak. '**YOU'RE BLESSED!**'

'**SHHHHH!**' hissed the crowds. Everyone wanted to hear what Jesus was going to say.

'To the poor, I say **HOORAY!** You're blessed – the kingdom of heaven belongs to you.

'To those who are hungry, I say **HOORAY!** You're blessed, and you'll eat till you're full up.

'To those who are crying, I say **HOORAY!** You're blessed, and you'll have the last laugh.'

'**HOORAY!**' shouted the crowds of poor, hungry, sad people who were following Jesus.

Then Jesus looked hard at his freshly picked team of disciples and said, 'When people hate you because of me; when you are excluded, insulted and rejected for my sake – **HOORAY!** Celebrate and jump for joy! You'll get a big reward in heaven. The prophets were treated in just the same way.' The disciples gulped. They knew the dangers those prophets had faced.*

Bad news – booo!

But Jesus hadn't finished. He could see some familiar faces amongst the ordinary people in the crowd: the wealthy Pharisees (those proud protectors of the Jewish religion) were strutting around in their fine robes, keeping him under surveillance. Some well-fed noblemen had come to see what all the fuss was about: they looked as fat and sleek as spoilt cats. Roman soldiers were standing guard like riot police, keeping an eye on the rabble. They were laughing and joking with each other.

Jesus continued in a loud voice, 'But to the rich, I say **BOOO!** You've already got an easy life.

* For example, you can read about the dangers faced by Elijah and Elisha in *On fire* in **Beastly Bible Stories 1**.

'To those who have full bellies, I say **BOOO!** You'll starve.

'To those who are laughing now, I say **BOOO!** It will be your turn to cry.

'When people praise you – **BOOO!** That's what they did to the false prophets.'

'BOOOO!' jeered the crowds, pointing at the rich Pharisees and the fat noblemen and the chuckling soldiers. They were happy to hear anything that was bad news for that lot!

Fighting talk

The crowds grew even more excited as people wondered whether Jesus was about to declare war on these important and powerful people. 'Will he take over the Temple, d'you think?' one man asked his neighbour.

'Will he crown himself king?' asked a woman.

'Will he run this country instead of the Romans?' asked a teenager. This was a popular idea and it caught on fast. People dreamt of seeing the Romans ruined: imagine if all those big bullies could be defeated in battle! Imagine Jesus, like Samson, squashing thousands of Israel's enemies!*

Jesus hollered like a head teacher above the hubbub. 'But **I'M TALKING** to everyone who's **LISTENING!**'

* You can read the bloodthirsty stories of Samson in **Beastly Bible Stories 1** and **2**.

'**SSHHHH!**' Silence fell, and everyone waited to hear what he'd say next.

'LOVE YOUR ENEMIES.'

????!! thought the crowds.

'Help anyone who hurts you,' continued Jesus. 'Bless anyone who curses you. Pray for anyone who threatens you. If someone slaps your cheek, offer him your other cheek too. If someone steals your coat, don't forget to give him your shirt as well. Give to everyone who begs from you. If anyone takes your stuff, don't ask for it back. Treat other people the way you'd like them to treat you.'

People stood with their mouths open. They'd liked the stuff about rich people getting nothing in the end and poor, hungry folk like them getting a feast in God's kingdom, but this was different. Let people steal from you and push you around? *Love* your *enemies?* They had never heard anything like it – and many of them didn't like it.

Jesus explained, 'If you only love people who love you back, so what? Big deal – even sinners do that. If you only do good to people who do good to you, so what? Like I say – even sinners do that. If you only lend money to people who will pay you back, don't expect God to be impressed. Sinners do that all the time. But **LOVE YOUR ENEMIES**, do good and lend even if you don't expect to get anything in return. You'll get a big reward, and what's

more you'll be God's own children – because he's kind to everyone, however bad or ungrateful they are.'

What would you have thought, if you'd been in the crowd that day? Would you have carried on following Jesus and admiring his miracles, or would you have thought he was asking too much? Jesus' disciples didn't have a choice – Jesus had chosen them and now they were all in it together.

> *When Jesus said, 'Love your enemies,' he was telling an important truth about God, who loves everyone, no matter who they are. However, for his followers it was one of the most shocking things this surprising Saviour ever said. Do you remember how the prophets had promised God's people a Saviour who would put everything right? Do you remember how Mary celebrated when she knew she was expecting Jesus, because she could see that God was going to keep his promise? She said, 'He'll put powerful people in their place! He'll help the hungry! He'll save us all!' John the Baptiser's dad was even more excited about the Saviour: he said, 'He'll be a battle-winning hero who will save us all! He'll show our enemies who's boss!'* As more and more people came to believe that Jesus really was the promised Saviour, this was the kind of hero they expected him to be. They certainly didn't expect him to say, 'Love your enemies'!*

You can read this story in Luke 6:12-35. There is similar teaching in Matthew 5–7.

* You can read about what Mary and Zechariah expected of Jesus in *Awesome angels* in **Beastly Bible Stories 5**.

'EAT MY BODY; DRINK MY BLOOD'

Jesus shocks his followers

Unfriended and unfollowed

No one was more popular than Jesus. People walked all day to see him, they stood in the sun to hear him and they risked getting trampled on just to touch him. His fans and followers couldn't get enough of his miracles, and when he fed 5000 of them with nothing but a small packed lunch, everyone celebrated.*

The crowds cheered, 'He's God's Chosen One! **THREE CHEERS FOR JESUS!**'

However, the very next day many fans changed their minds. '**DISGUSTING!**' they cried. '**OUTRAGEOUS!!** There's **NO WAY** I'm following **HIM!!!**' Hundreds of them stomped off in a huff. What on earth had happened? Jesus' troublemaking teaching, that's what . . .

---

* You can read this story in *The all-you-can-eat picnic* in **Beastly Bible Stories 5**.

The bread of life

After the miraculous all-you-can-eat picnic, everyone was looking for Jesus. You and I know he was busy bossing a storm about, but when the crowds eventually found him in the synagogue in Capernaum, they bombarded him with questions, beginning with, 'Where *were* you?'

Jesus snapped back, 'You're only looking for me now because yesterday you pigged out on miraculous bread!' Some people looked embarrassed: how had Jesus known they were hoping for more free food? He continued, 'Don't work for food that goes off – instead, focus on the bread that will last forever! That's what the Son of God is offering you!'

The crowds licked their lips. Their tummies were still rumbling and they liked the sound of this special bread. They shouted, '**GIVE US IT**! We want the bread you're talking about!'

Then Jesus took the lesson to the next level. '**I AM THE BREAD OF LIFE**,' he said. 'If you come to me, you'll never be hungry again, and if you believe in me, you'll never be thirsty. I have come down from heaven so that everyone who sees me and believes in me will live forever. This is what God wants.'

The crowds were amazed. Some got the point straight away and felt full up with faith: they believed in Jesus, they knew they had to follow him and they trusted that they'd live forever. Others were confused and upset: those who had hoped for a handout of heavenly bread muttered about being hungry, and many Jews in the synagogue couldn't believe their ears when Jesus said, 'I have come down from heaven.'

'**HIM?!**' they cried. 'But he's Joseph the builder's son! We know his family! How can he say he came down from heaven?!'

Jesus cut across the mumbling and grumbling. '**STOP MOANING!**' he shouted. 'Everyone who listens properly to God comes to me. And the ones who believe in me **WILL** live forever. Listen: **I AM** the bread of life. **THIS**,' (he pointed at himself) 'is the bread from heaven that you can eat, and then live forever. For the sake of the whole world, the bread I'm giving you is my flesh.'

Well, what would *you* think? Lots of Jews in the synagogue heard Jesus' words – 'The bread I'm giving you is my flesh' – and nearly fainted in disgust. They looked at Jesus and shuddered, 'What does he think we are – **CANNIBALS?!**' They imagined tucking in to Jesus' hairy legs and felt sick. 'How can we eat his flesh?! The very idea!'

Jesus continued over the uproar, 'I'm telling you that unless you eat the Son of God's flesh and drink his blood, you won't live. Anyone who scoffs my flesh and slurps my blood will have eternal life!'

YUCK! The crowds in the synagogue reeled in shock. They had never heard anything like this before. '**DISGUSTING!**' they cried. '**OUTRAGEOUS!!** There's **NO WAY** I'm following **HIM!!!**' Hundreds of fans stomped off in a huff. They didn't want to have anything more to do with Jesus.

Jesus watched them go. He could hear the rest of his followers muttering amongst themselves. 'This is tough stuff,' they complained. 'How can anyone listen to such sick lessons?'

'Oh, have I offended you?' Jesus asked them. They looked shiftily at each other. They were still trying to get their heads around Jesus' teaching. He explained, 'I'm actually talking about **LIFE** – but not all of you believe me.' (Jesus always knew what his disciples were thinking: he knew who didn't believe him and he even knew who was going to betray him in the end.) Many followers decided to unfollow Jesus – they simply turned their backs on him and walked away.

The disciples' decision

Then Jesus turned to his 12 special disciples* and said, 'What about you? Do you want to leave, too?'

* He chose them in the last story – *Love your enemies!*

The men looked at each other, and Simon Peter replied, 'Who else are we going to follow? You're the one who's talking about eternal life. We believe and know that you're the Holy One of God.' The disciples nodded.

Jesus said, 'Didn't I choose you all – my task force – my Twelve? But one of you is a devil.' He was talking about Judas Iscariot – keep your eye on him from now on . . .

This story shows some of Jesus' most troublemaking teaching. Many people at the time took his words literally and really thought that Jesus wanted them to be cannibals! No wonder they gave up following him. In fact, Jesus was talking about the importance of believing in him. People relied on bread to stay alive, so when Jesus said he was 'the Bread of Life', he meant that faith in him is even more vital and eternally life-giving than this everyday bread. Here is the simplest way of explaining it: JESUS = LIFE.

Following the events of the Last Supper,* Christians have understood that when Jesus talks about eating his flesh and drinking his blood, he is talking about the bread and wine we eat and drink in church as part of Holy Communion. Here's what the Bible tells us about the Last Supper:

* You can read about this in *Extraordinary Easter* in **Beastly Bible Stories 7**.

While they were eating, Jesus took a loaf of bread, and after blessing it he broke it, gave it to the disciples, and said, 'Take, eat; this is my body.' Then he took a cup, and after giving thanks he gave it to them, saying, 'Drink from it, all of you; for this is my blood of the covenant, which is poured out for many for the forgiveness of sins.'

Matthew 26:26-28

This bread and wine represent Jesus' body and blood that he sacrificed for us all on the cross.

You can read this story in John 6:22-71.

TOPSY TURVY
God's upside-down kingdom

Rich man, poor man

The young man stood out from the crowd like a flamingo among a flock of pigeons. He walked towards Jesus, past the poor and hungry people whose rags were held together by dirt, in his fine white linen tunic and gorgeous blue cloak with gold fringes. His clean hair was oiled and curled. His face shone. As he walked, he handed out coins to the beggars around him, carefully reaching into a pouch he always kept for that purpose. It was important, he knew, to give a little something to the poor.

'Look at him – he's as rich as a king!' whispered a boy.

'God must really love him,' said his mum.

The boy's dad grabbed one of the coins and said, 'He's flashing his cash – you can see how God has blessed him!' It seemed obvious to everyone in the crowd that if you were rich, like this young man, then you were one of God's favourites and on the fast track to heaven.

The young man had a question for Jesus. He wanted to know how to get his hands on one of the few things he didn't yet own. 'Teacher,' he asked, 'what good deed should I do so that I can get eternal life?'

Jesus replied, 'If you want eternal life, you've got to keep the commandments.'

'Which ones?' the young man asked.

' "Do not kill", "Do not steal", "Don't tell lies" – you know, the Big Ten.'*

'Oh *those*,' replied the young man. 'I've kept all *them* since I was a kid. What else?'

Jesus looked him straight in the eyes. 'If you want to be perfect, go, sell all your possessions and give all the money to the poor. There'll be treasure for you in heaven. Then come and follow me.'

Well, what would you do? The young man gulped. He was gutted. Sell all his stuff? What about his cool clothes and his handsome house and his fine furniture? What about his jewellery? How could he do without it all? How could he give all his money to the poor people around him? Then he'd be poor, like them! The more he thought about it, the sicker he felt. He walked away from Jesus, shaking his head.

Then Jesus said to his disciples, 'See? It's hard for a rich person to get into heaven. It's easier for a camel to squeeze through the eye of a needle than it is for someone rich to make it into God's kingdom.'

* You can read about the Ten Commandments in *Laws for living* in **Beastly Bible Stories 2**.

Jesus' disciples stood with their mouths open, like landed fish. Their brains were trying to take in a brand-new idea: rich people weren't God's favourites, after all! 'But –' they asked, 'in that case, who on earth *is* going to get into heaven?'

Jesus replied, 'It's impossible for human beings, but for God – everything is possible!'

Peter panicked. Was Jesus changing all the rules? He thought of his fishing boat and his carefully mended nets, and how he had left them all beside Lake Galilee. Was it all for nothing? 'Look, Lord, we never had much, but we gave it all up to follow you!' He looked round at his fellow fishermen. 'What about us? What will we get?'

Jesus replied, 'I promise – when the Son of God sits on his throne of glory in heaven, you 12 who have followed me will sit on 12 thrones. And everyone who has left their family or friends or livelihood for my sake will be rewarded a hundred times over and will have eternal life.' At this, Peter and the other disciples breathed a huge sigh of relief. 'But,' continued Jesus, 'many people who are in first place now will be last – and many others who are at the bottom of the heap now will be in the place of honour in heaven.'

Flash forward: Jesus predicts his death

Then Jesus called his 12 disciples to a secret meeting. He told them what no one else knew except him and God: 'Look, we're heading for Jerusalem, and the Son of God will be handed over to the chief priests and the scribes, and they will sentence him to death. Then they will give him up to the Romans, who will bully him and whip him and kill him on a cross. Then, on the third day, he will be raised up.'

Just like that – he told them how he was going to die! It was horrible – and it sounded as if it would be soon! As for the 'raised up' part, no one was quite sure what that meant. The disciples looked at each other and thought of a hundred questions. *Why?* they wondered. *When will this happen? What can we do to stop it? What will happen to us?* But they didn't dare ask anything.

First and last

Later that day, two of the disciples weren't thinking about Jesus at all. James and John, the Thunder Boys, were arguing about the places of honour in heaven. They liked the sound of the best throne. '**THAT'S MINE!**' said James, and pushed his brother. '**NO – IT'S MINE!**' shouted John, and shoved him back.

The Thunder Boys' mum, who had seen them fight like this since they were kids, tried to sort things out before they started to punch each other. She dragged them both to Jesus and said, 'Can I ask a favour? Say that both these sons of mine will sit in the places of honour in your kingdom – one on each side of you!'

Jesus looked at the red-faced, furious brothers and said, 'You don't know what you're asking for. Can you follow me where I'm going?'

'**YES!**' answered the Thunder Boys together.

'Yes, you will,' said Jesus, 'but as for the places of honour in heaven – that's not up to me. God decides that.'

Just then, the other ten disciples stomped up and gave the Thunder Boys a shove.

'**PLACE OF HONOUR, EH?**' snarled Andrew.

'Need your mummy's help? Aw, diddums!' sneered Bartholomew.

'Think you're better than the rest of us, do you? **PAH!**' scoffed Thomas.

Jesus shouted, '**HEY!** This is how the rest of the world behaves – trying to be top dog and lording it over all the rest. You're supposed to be different! If you want to be Mr Big, you've got to be a servant, and if you want the place of honour you've got to be the humblest slave. Follow my example: God's Son didn't come to be waited on hand and foot, but to work as a servant, and to give up his life for other people's sake.'

Jesus carried on walking towards Jerusalem, but as they followed him the disciples felt wobbly, as if they were losing their balance. First they had learned that rich men didn't automatically get into heaven, and now they – the select few – had been told to be slaves! In God's kingdom, the first were going to be last and the last were going to be first: the disciples felt as if their world was turning upside down.

This troublesome teaching turned upside down the things that people thought they knew. It is one more example of how different Jesus was, and shows why many people found it difficult to understand and accept him. At this point, his disciples were struggling. They must have asked themselves, 'How can God's Son be a servant?' and 'How can the Saviour end up being killed by the Romans?' But Jesus – the Surprising Saviour – continued to say and do things that no one expected . . .

You can read this story in Matthew 19:16-30 and 20:17-28.

TRASHING THE TEMPLE
Jesus puts his foot down

Going to God's house

Do you remember the time when Jesus got lost, when he was 12 years old?* His mum and dad found him in the Temple in Jerusalem, but Jesus didn't feel lost at all. He felt at home, because the Temple was God's house – his Father's house. Whenever Jesus and his disciples went back to Jerusalem, they always visited the Temple first. For every Jew, it was the holiest place on earth. For Jesus, it was like going home.

Imagine going there yourself! Picture yourself in Jerusalem, 2000 years ago. You can't miss the great Temple: its towering walls are built of shining white stone, and its grand gateways, steep steps and cool colonnades make you feel as though you are walking into heaven itself. Imagine! But as you walk through the first gateway, you find yourself in a paved courtyard that sounds and smells more like a farmyard.

* You can read this story in *Missing Messiah* in **Beastly Bible Stories 5**.

93

'BAAAAAA! BAAAAAA! BAAAAAA!'
'MOOOOOOOOO! MOOOOOOOOO!'

The hot, grassy smell of dung is so strong that you can almost taste it. **YUCK!** Watch your step – there are cowpats and sheep droppings everywhere. Calves and lambs are being led or carried into the next courtyard – it's just as well they don't know what's waiting for them around the corner! (An altar for animal sacrifice and a priest with a big knife, that's what.)*

Imagine! There are bird cages covered in crusty white droppings, full of anxiously flapping doves. But there's more than animals and birds and noise and stink: money is changing hands around you faster than in a supermarket on a Saturday morning. Every pilgrim who comes to the Temple has to pay a tax with a special coin, so everyone is changing their own cash for Temple tokens. Walk carefully through the crowds so that you don't bump into anyone's stall! Money-changers stand guard over teetering towers of coins and delicate balancing scales. Don't trust them: their hands move fast, like magicians doing card tricks, and it's not always easy to check the coins they give you before they're waving at another customer and shouting, '**NEXT!**'

Imagine the racket! Everyone around you is trying to seal a deal, make a quick sale, haggle for a bargain or argue for a refund. You could be in a street

* You can read more about animal sacrifice in *Blood and guts* in **Beastly Bible Stories 2**.

94

market, a shopping mall or an everything-must-go sale – not in God's Temple at all.

Clearing up and clearing out

Jesus was used to these scenes in the Temple – the market was bigger, noisier and more cut-throat every time he visited – but on this particular day, he decided to put his foot down. All these tradesmen and tricksters had been trashing the Temple for long enough, and his Father's house needed a serious spring clean.

First he grabbed some rope and made it into a whip. He said to his disciples, 'Stand back!'

WHAP! WHAP! WHAP! He smacked the whip around and drove all the sheep and cows out of the Temple, followed by their wailing owners. **CHINK CHINK CHINK CHINK CHINK!** He chucked all the money-changers' carefully collected coins on the ground and pushed their tables over: **SMASH! CRASH! BASH!** Their scales broke – **CLANG DINK!** – and their money rolled all over the place. People scrambled to pick it up and pocket it. Then Jesus kicked over the dove-sellers' stools – **CLUNK! THUNK!** – and yelled at them, '**GET OUT OF HERE!** Stop treating my Father's house like a farmer's market!'

The cattle merchants and the shepherds and the dove-sellers and the money-changers were outraged: 'WHAT DO YOU THINK YOU'RE DOING?!'

'WHO'S GOING TO ROUND UP MY SHEEP?'

'OY! THOSE WERE MY DOVES!'

'GIMME BACK MY MONEY!'

Above the yelling, Jesus shouted, 'GOD SAID, "MY HOUSE IS A PLACE FOR PRAYER." YOU LOT HAVE MADE IT A HIDEOUT FOR ROBBERS AND RIP-OFF MERCHANTS!'

Murder in mind

There was uproar in the Temple. Suddenly the place looked different: the animals and the money-changers had gone, and the people who had always been kept outside the gates – those who couldn't see or walk – came hobbling and crawling towards Jesus. He dropped his whip and gently put his hands on them: they were instantly, miraculously cured. Blind people looked around and saw the Temple for the first time in their lives; lame people danced and jumped for joy. Kids raced around Jesus and yelled the praise they'd heard other people shouting: 'Hosanna to the Son of David!'

Silently watching all this celebration were the chief priests and the scribes. They were scowling: the Temple was *their* place, and *they* were in charge – who did Jesus think he was, to change the way things had always been? They looked at the hysterical crowds and saw how they hung on his every word. The priests were terrified of the power that Jesus had over the people, so together they plotted and planned to get rid of him for good. Somehow, they were going to kill this troublemaking teacher.

Did you know that Jesus got this angry? Did you know that he made such a mess in the Temple and upset so many people? He really is the surprising Saviour! He did all this to make God's Temple the special place for prayer that it was always meant to be, but the chief priests who were in charge thought he was just causing trouble. No wonder they were afraid and wanted to kill him. Read on for their TOP SECRET files on Jesus and his disciples . . . You can find out how their murderous plot turns out in the next book: **Beastly Bible Stories 7 – Gory, gory hallelujah!**

You can read this story in Matthew 21:12-17, Mark 11:15-19, Luke 19:45-48 and John 2:13-16.

JERUSALEM'S MOST WANTED

POLICE FILE

NAME: Jesus of Nazareth ALSO KNOWN AS: King of the Jews, Son of God, Messiah, Teacher

OCCUPATION: Teacher and preacher, former builder

CAUTION: Jesus is known for performing dramatic and disturbing miracles: local people even claim that he has raised a man from the dead. His preaching has been known to offend the public. He openly defies religious authority and breaks the Sabbath. He can be violent – he recently destroyed a market in the Temple. Responsible for the death of 2000 pigs in Gerasa. Very popular, always surrounded by crowds of hysterical followers. Public arrest may spark riots.

NAME: Simon Peter A.K.A: Peter, The Rock

OCCUPATION: Follower of Jesus, former fisherman

CAUTION: Jesus' right-hand man. Passionate, unstable, often acts on impulse and has emotional outbursts. Unpredictable – may become violent if challenged.

NAME: Andrew A.K.A: The Rock's brother

OCCUPATION: Follower of Jesus, former fisherman

CAUTION: Loyal to his brother Simon Peter.
Former follower of known troublemaker John the
Baptiser (recently executed).

NAME: James A.K.A: Thunder Boy

OCCUPATION: Follower of Jesus, former fisherman

CAUTION: Close to Jesus. Extremely fiery temper,
may be violent and unpredictable.

NAME: John A.K.A: Thunder Boy

OCCUPATION: Follower of Jesus, former fisherman

CAUTION: Brother of James. Very close to Jesus.

Extremely fiery temper, may be violent and

unpredictable. Good with words – an influential follower.

NAME: Philip A.K.A: 'The fixer'

OCCUPATION: Follower of Jesus

CAUTION: Close to Simon Peter and Andrew. A practical man – can

estimate costs quickly (e.g. feeding 5000 people at short notice).

NAME: Bartholomew A.K.A: Nathanael, 'The straight talker'

OCCUPATION: Follower of Jesus

CAUTION: Likes plain speaking. Overheard by witnesses at his first meeting with Jesus of Nazareth: 'Since when did anything good come out of Nazareth?'

NAME: Thomas A.K.A: 'The realist'

OCCUPATION: Follower of Jesus

CAUTION: Devoted follower – prepared to die in Jesus' service. Thinks literally, likes facts and hard evidence.

NAME: Matthew A.K.A: Levi, 'The money-grabber'

OCCUPATION: Follower of Jesus, former tax collector

CAUTION: An unpopular follower who associates with traitors and thieves.

NAME: Judas A.K.A: 'The thief'

OCCUPATION: Follower of Jesus, treasurer for the group

CAUTION: Known to be dishonest. Not to be trusted with money. May be less loyal to Jesus than the rest. One to watch.

NAME: James A.K.A: son of Alphaeus, James the Younger

OCCUPATION: Follower of Jesus

CAUTION: Little is known about him – more surveillance needed.

NAME: Thaddeus A.K.A: Judas son of James

OCCUPATION: Follower of Jesus

CAUTION: Little is known about him – more surveillance needed.

NAME: Simon A.K.A: Simon the Zealot

OCCUPATION: Follower of Jesus

CAUTION: A known anti-Roman activist with a violent past. Could be dangerous.

OTHER KNOWN ASSOCIATES: Mary of Nazareth; Lazarus, Mary and Martha of Bethany; Zacchaeus the tax collector; local Roman Centurion; Jairus the synagogue leader; numerous lepers, sinners and local people.